◎ Contents

KT-104-533

◎ What is a bunker?

During the bombing raids of World War II (1939–45), people needed safe places to go. One of these was a bunker: a reinforced underground shelter. In Britain, the Prime Minister and his government ran the country from a bunker in London.

Why did they build bunkers and shelters?

From the very beginning of the war, people believed the Luftwaffe (German Air Force) would launch bombing raids on some European cities – making it easier for Germany to invade. The British government planned bunkers and shelters to keep civilian casualties as low as possible.

JUNE 1938	27 AUGUST 1939	1 SEPTEMBER 1939	3 SEPTEMBER 1939

Work begins on the government bunker and also on brick and concrete street shelters.	The government bunker, later called the Cabinet War Rooms, is ready.	Germany invades Poland – a country Britain had agreed to protect.	World War II begins. People use stations on the London Underground as air-raid shelters.

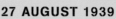

What bunkers and bomb shelters were there in World War II?

The British government quickly supplied shelters that people could use in their garden. They also built public street shelters. Even natural caves and London's Tube stations became safe havens from German air raids.

◁ Members of the public had access to street shelters like this one.

"You can't sleep there!"

▲ Initially, people were not encouraged to sleep in Tube stations.

Where was the government's bunker?

The government's underground bunker was in Whitehall, at 1 Storey's Gate, within easy reach of both the Prime Minister's home and office at 10 Downing Street, and the Houses of Parliament. Its secret location near St James's Park was known only to a few people, even after the war.

▲ Anderson shelters were built in gardens and saved hundreds of lives.

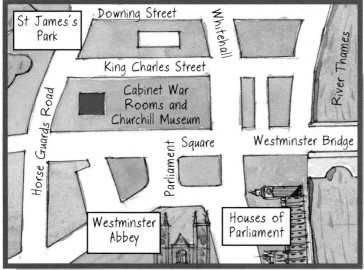

The bunker is still under the building at 1 Storey's Gate on Horse Guards Road and King Charles Street. It is now part of a museum.

When was the government's bunker built?

Government officials began planning defences, bunkers and shelters well before the war began. The main elements were in place by the time war broke out on 3 September 1939.

⊙ Why did Britain fight in the war?

After Germany lost World War I (1914–18) its economy was in ruins. In the 1930s, Adolf Hitler became Germany's new leader. He wanted to rebuild the nation's power and to control the rest of Europe.

Why did Britain fight Germany?

Hitler's German forces began to take over parts of Europe. Britain's Prime Minister, Neville Chamberlain, tried to make peace, even when Hitler's army took over Czechoslovakia. But Hitler continued to push German forces on their menacing path.

In September 1939, Germany invaded Poland, too – a country Britain had agreed to protect. So, on 3 September, Britain and France declared war on Germany. Soon after, Chamberlain resigned as Prime Minister and Winston Churchill took over.

Why did Germany want to attack Britain?

By the end of 1940, Germany's forces had invaded and overcome a large part of Europe. Only the USSR (the Communist Soviet Union centred around Russia) to the east and Britain in the west stood in the way. Hitler chose to attack Britain, a powerful country with a large empire. If Britain could be defeated it would give Germany command over Europe, and possibly the whole world.

WAR TIMELINE

(1) In 1940 Germany invades Norway, Denmark, Holland, Belgium and Luxembourg. When the German army invades France, British forces retreat to England from the coast at Dunkirk

(2) 1940 German U-boats begin attacking British ships in the Atlantic

(3) 1940 British forces fight Italian troops in North Africa

(4) December 1941 Japanese planes attack the USA's Pearl Harbor naval base in Hawaii

(5) 1941 The USA enters the war

(6) 1941 Germany invades the USSR, heading for Leningrad and Moscow

(7) 1941-2 Allied forces fight German forces in North Africa

(8) 1941-2 Japanese forces attack British territories in Asia (Hong Kong, Singapore, Malaysia, Burma (Myanmar) and Indonesia).

(9) Allied troops fight back

(10) 1942 Japanese and US forces fight in the Pacific

How did it grow into a world war?

The war quickly spread beyond Europe to Africa and Asia. Italy joined Germany and invaded North Africa. Later, Japanese forces attacked the US Pacific fleet at Pearl Harbor and British territories in Asia. Germany, Italy and Japan were called the Axis powers, and their actions made the conflict global.

The USA joined the war in December 1941, after Japan attacked Pearl Harbor. The USA declared war on Germany and Italy soon after. Britain's new Prime Minister, Winston Churchill, was pleased to have US President FD Roosevelt as his new ally.

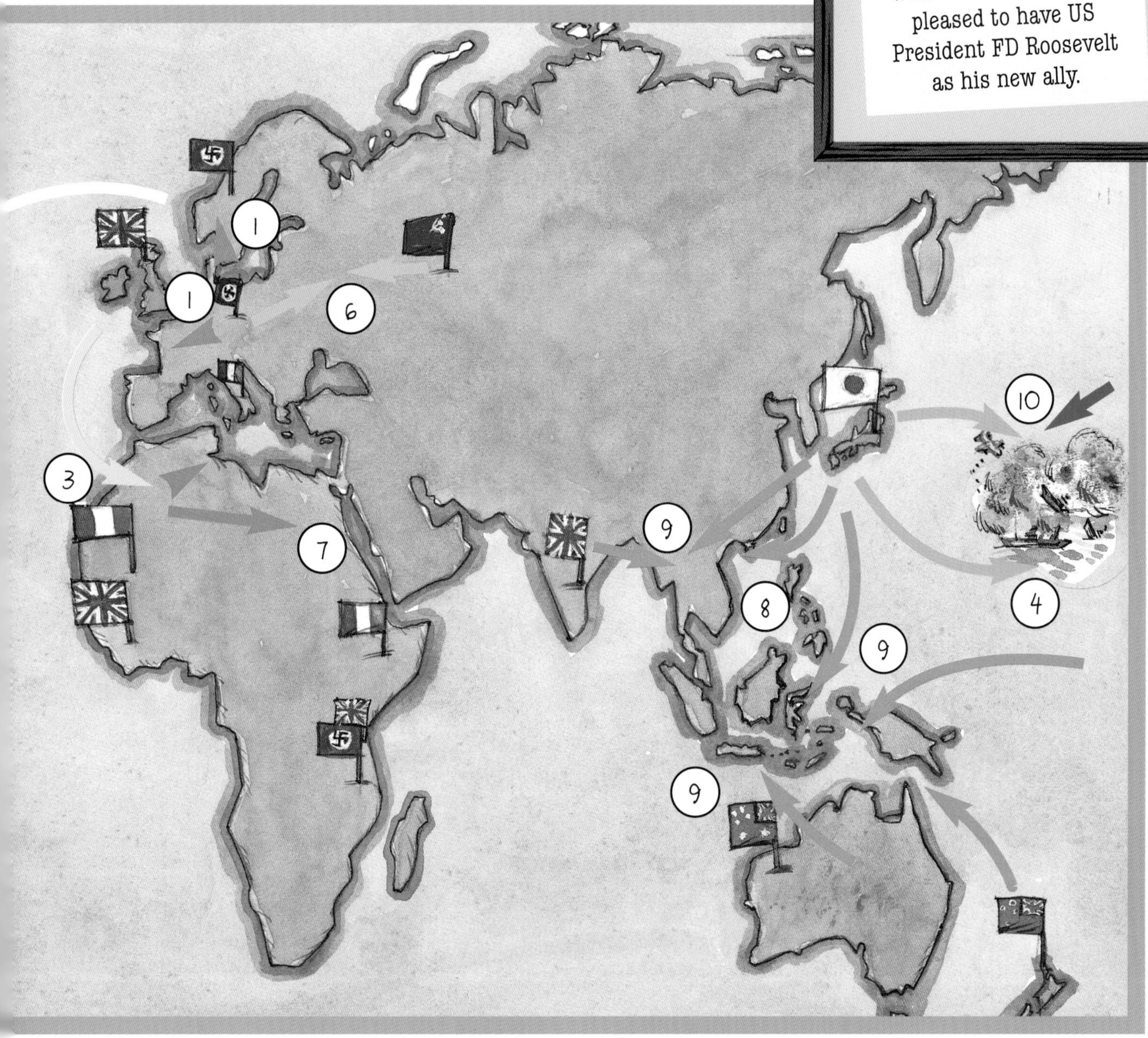

Countries from the British Empire joined in the fighting, sending troops to help, or defending themselves against attack.

India

Nigeria

Jamaica

Australia and New Zealand

Malaysia

⊙ Who needed protection?

Before the war began, politicians believed that German air raids could kill thousands of British people in the first weeks of the war. They were also worried that a German bomb would hit Whitehall, wiping out the country's leaders and creating chaos.

What was the Battle of Britain?

Starting in July 1940, Germany attempted to destroy the RAF (Royal Air Force) with bombing raids on British airfields, and in a series of aerial battles above south-east England. On 15 September Hitler launched a huge attack to finally crush the RAF. But the Luftwaffe suffered heavy losses and was defeated on what is now called Battle of Britain Day.

In 1939, 1.5 million children left big cities in a mass evacuation. Street shelters were built as the government prepared for war. 38 million gas masks were issued too, in case of a poison gas attack. Fortunately they were never needed.

What was the 'Blitz'?

The 'Blitz' (short for Blitzkrieg which means lightning strike) began on 24 August 1940 when German bombers dropped high explosives onto London. On 26 September 1940 a bomb actually hit Whitehall! The Blitz spread to other major British cities, but by October the Battle of Britain and the Blitz were over.

The British government feared casualties of over 200,000 after just one week of German air raids. In fact, bombs killed only 60,000 civilians in the whole course of the war.

THE WAR CABINET

What was the War Cabinet and why protect it?

By the time the Blitz started, the government's top secret bunker under Whitehall had been completed for over a year. It allowed the Prime Minister's War Cabinet, made up of top political advisers and military experts, to meet in relative safety. Together, the War Cabinet planned the defeat of Hitler and Germany.

Who was part of the War Cabinet?

Less than seven weeks after war was declared, Prime Minister Neville Chamberlain held his first ever Cabinet meeting in the bunker. But in May 1940, he was replaced by Winston Churchill, who became both Prime Minister and Minister of Defence. Key members of Churchill's War Cabinet included Neville Chamberlain, Clement Attlee and Arthur Greenwood, and Lord Halifax. The well-organised War Cabinet had overall responsibility for winning the war.

Winston Churchill – Prime Minister and Chairman of the War Cabinet. Churchill was a strong-willed man, often remembered for his habit of smoking a cigar. He was a man of action – just the sort of person needed to help win the war.

Neville Chamberlain – Lord President of the Council

Clement Attlee – Lord Privy Seal

Arthur Greenwood – Minister without Portfolio

Lord Halifax – Foreign Secretary

Sir Hastings Ismay – Chief of Staff

"C" – the unidentified spy chief

Other Cabinet ministers

Other Cabinet members

There were other members of the Cabinet, including Sir Hastings Ismay, "C" and other ministers. At the height of the war, eight people formed the War Cabinet.

◎ What were the War Rooms like?

The bunker, later called the Cabinet War Rooms (CWRs), was created from a maze of basement storerooms under a Whitehall office building.

Who planned the bunker?

In 1938, Sir Hastings Ismay and Major Leslie Hollis set to work planning the transformation of the basement into a top-secret bunker. For six years and for 24 hours a day, it would be a home for politicians, military personnel and their support staff.

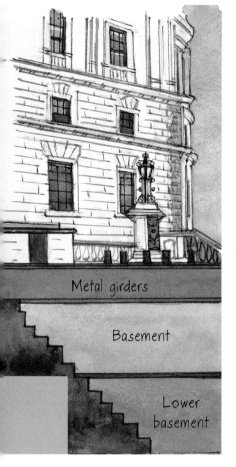

Metal girders

Basement

Lower basement

◀ The basement had two levels and a roof supported by metal girders.

The entrance to the bunker was inside the building at 1 Storey's Gate: the offices of the Board of Trade. ▶

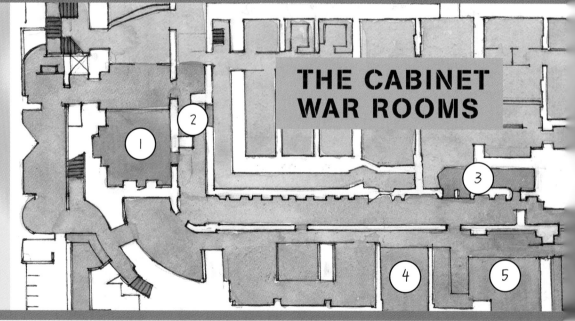

A plan of the bunker (Cabinet War Rooms):
1. Cabinet Room (page 14)
2. Entrance to the "Dock" (page 15)
3. Transatlantic Telephone Room (page 21)
4. Churchill's quarters (page 14)
5. Central Map Room (pages 18–19)

THE CABINET WAR ROOMS

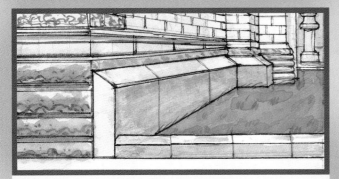

To protect against bomb blasts above ground, a concrete "apron" was built around the base of the building. But it went only one metre underground!

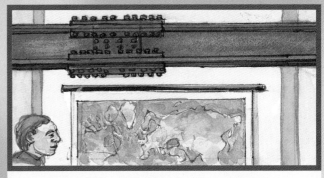

One of the reasons the basement was chosen was because it already had thick metal girders supporting the building.

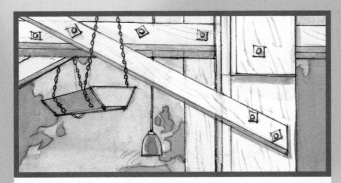

Some rooms were reinforced with wooden beams and trusses. In places there were so many that people had to mind their heads.

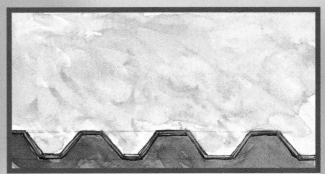

Initially, the CWRs were too weak, so engineers built a one-metre thick, concrete and girder roof above them that became known as the "slab".

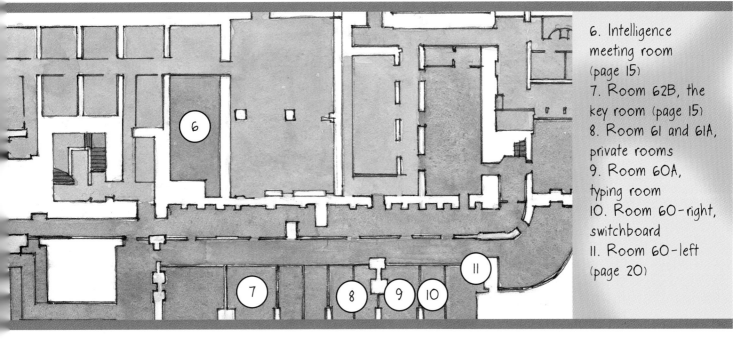

6. Intelligence meeting room (page 15)
7. Room 62B, the key room (page 15)
8. Room 61 and 61A, private rooms
9. Room 60A, typing room
10. Room 60-right, switchboard
11. Room 60-left (page 20)

◎ What happened in the Rooms?

There were many rooms in the bunker. Probably the most important were the Central Map Room, the Cabinet Room, and Churchill's comfortable office and private quarters. However, Churchill often preferred to stay above ground.

"This is the room from which I will direct the war."

Cabinet Room

Churchill held 115 Cabinet meetings here. The room was quite small, with tables, maps and a clock on the wall. The War Cabinet met here at any time of day or night. Churchill had his own wooden chair, and kept his official papers in a red box.

Central Map Room

Few people were allowed into the Central Map Room. It had a huge map on the wall, showing where fighting was taking place around the world. Letters and coloured telephones (see page 21) brought news of the war that officers plotted on the map and logged in the records.

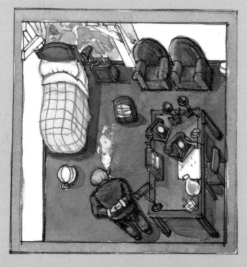

Churchill's quarters

This had a desk, a map of Western Europe and a bed in it. Churchill rarely slept here though, preferring to stay above ground. There was an ashtray for his cigar, two telephones (a green one for secret, "scrambled" conversations) and microphones for broadcasting speeches.

Key room

From 1941, all the keys to the Cabinet War Rooms were kept in Room 62B, under the watchful eye of the so-called "Camp Commandant", Lawrence Burgis.

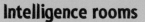

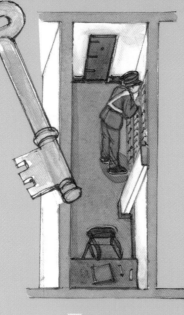

Intelligence rooms

Room 59 was for the Joint Planning Staff, and the mysterious "C" used adjoining rooms. His work became very important as the war progressed.

Switchboards and offices

Typists and telephonists worked day and night in the Cabinet War Rooms. There was a room-sized switchboard where staff preferred to sleep by their phones – instead of in the Dock (see below). The offices were cramped and subdivided, so they never had enough space.

Churchill's and Ismay's private secretaries' rooms

These senior civil servants and military men stayed in the cramped, partitioned Rooms 61 and 61A. They were Churchill's and Ismay's right-hand men. Their jobs were to make the Cabinet and military committees run smoothly.

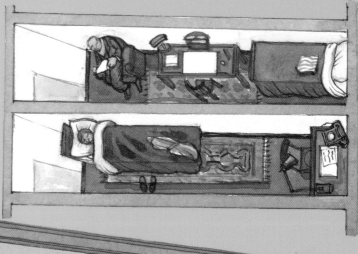

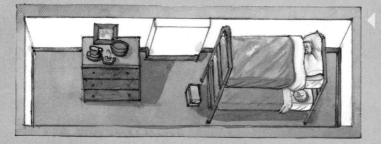

The Dock

The Dock was the name given to the cramped lower basement reached through a trapdoor. It was used as a dormitory for secretaries, clerks and junior staff, but was two floors below the nearest women's toilet!

◉ What was it like for the staff?

Many people down in the Cabinet War Rooms didn't really know what was happening above ground, but there were ways of getting information to them. Lights over doorways signalled an air raid, a bell outside the Cabinet Room warned of other dangers above – and a sign gave a brief weather forecast.

What happened during an air raid?

Work continued normally during air raids. In the senior staff's private rooms, in the Prime Minister's suite and in the Cabinet Room, buttons and wires connected to the rooms of the junior staff. When the button was pressed the juniors could be summoned in a moment.

Did they have blackouts underground?

Because no light could escape to attract German bomber planes above, the underground rooms had no need to worry about the nightly "blackout". But – just like the public – politicians and military personnel in the bunker still had to carry gas masks everywhere they went, in case of a poison gas attack.

▲ Signs were used to tell people about air raids.

The junior officials and support staff

The bunker's support and junior staff had a very uncomfortable time sleeping underground in the Dock. They had to put up with cold concrete floors and very hard metal beds. But after their 16-hour shift, they couldn't always find a spare bed! Some people preferred to go home for breaks rather than endure the prison-like conditions.

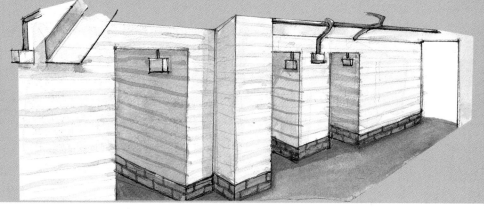

I'm so tired! But we must do everything we can to win the war.

Secretaries and telephonists

These shift-workers were vital to the smooth running of the Cabinet War Rooms. Many had to stay on duty as long as there was work to be done, in rooms filled with dust from the bombing.

Soldiers

A few Royal Marines armed with rifles stayed underground at all times, to guard the Cabinet War Rooms.

Detectives

Private detectives protected the Prime Minister 24 hours a day, staying in a basic room near Churchill's quarters.

17

◎ How did they follow the war?

The Central Map Room was the bunker's nerve centre. Here, officers logged details of British convoys in the Atlantic Ocean, German U-boats, and information from the world's war fronts – including Germany's Russian front. All these details were plotted on a huge wall map using pins, labels and woollen thread.

Coastal RADAR detects approaching Luftwaffe planes

Operations rooms pass on "filtered" information

Aircraft take photographs of enemy positions

How did officers gather information?

Information came into the Central Map Room by various routes. Five officers sat at the main table, ready to answer telephones, check letters, update the information on the maps – and pass it on to Churchill, the Chief of Staff and the King. There was one man each for the Royal Navy, RAF, Army and Home Guard – and also a Duty Officer.

The French Resistance (people in France secretly fighting the German occupation) send reports about weapons and enemy positions

British spies send intelligence reports from around the world

The coloured telephones – ringing almost continuously – connected the officers to different areas of the Cabinet War Rooms, or outside to 10 Downing Street.

Russia sends reports from the Eastern front (from 1941)

US ships and planes in the Pacific send reports (from 1941)

Ships on the North Atlantic front send telegraph messages – and later report German U-boat positions

In the Map Room Annexe next door, other officers plotted Hitler's advances and retreats, ready to inform the Prime Minister and his military staff – and charted British casualty statistics from German attacks.

British forces on the North African front (from 1940) send updates

They used the annexe's "scrambler" telephone for secret calls to offices around the bunker (see page 20).

The day will come when the joybells will ring again throughout Europe...

Churchill loved maps, and often visited the Central Map Room to check on the war's progress.

◎ How did people communicate?

The Cabinet War Rooms were a vital part of the government's wartime centre of information, so they needed the latest technology to provide quick and secure communications.

Why did they have four post collections per day?

In the 1940s, email didn't exist, so people relied on other forms of communication, such as the post. To help pass on letters and other up-to-date information quickly, the Cabinet War Rooms had its post collected and delivered four times a day.

Why did they use telegrams?

Telegrams were useful for short but important messages, and were one of the quickest ways to send information during World War II. Using telegraph handsets, the messages were sent along a wire, converted at the receiving end from electrical signals into writing, and then delivered – all in the space of a few minutes.

Churchill made four historic speeches from the Cabinet War Rooms in the years 1940–41, including the famous one that offered "blood, toil, tears and sweat" before Britain could win the war.

Why did the BBC install radio equipment?

The BBC put radio broadcasting equipment in tiny Room 60 from where Churchill could speak to Britain, Europe and the Commonwealth. Wires also led to microphones in the Prime Minister's quarters.

Green telephones were "scrambled" for intelligence reports

Black telephones connected to the switchboard

White telephones connected to other service rooms

An ivory telephone connected to 10 Downing Street

What were "scrambler" telephones?

Scrambler telephones were used for top-secret calls. They jumbled up the speakers' voices so that enemy spies, who might be listening in, could not understand the conversation.

What were the message tubes for?

Post Office vacuum message tubes were introduced to the Central Map Room in 1940. Amazingly, compressed air could propel documents from one end of the Cabinet War Rooms to the other, in seconds!

Hey, that was quick! Thanks!

What was the Transatlantic Telephone?

Churchill's special Transatlantic Telephone was in an old box room originally used to store brooms. From here he could speak to the US President on a secure "scrambled" phone line. From mid-1943 it used the secret and very complex "Sigsaly" equipment from the USA – installed on the other side of London because it was so big!

◉ How did the war change life?

When war began in 1939, life was turned upside down. Most of the country's young men went off to war, leaving women to take over their work. Many children in cities were evacuated to the countryside.

How did people's lives change?
During the war people couldn't take anything for granted. Their home, family or neighbourhood was at risk from bombing. Life changed very quickly.

Young city children were evacuated. They were sent to live with strangers in the countryside, away from the city.

Men of fighting age were conscripted into the Forces.

Women took over some jobs from men. Many became air-raid wardens.

Some joined the land army and helped grow food.

Other women became entertainers to keep morale high.

We have labels so people know our names.

We can do the same work a man does.

Why did people try to carry on as usual?

Air raids interrupted work and the government introduced rationing to prevent supplies running out, but people got used to their wartime life. They knew sacrifices had to be made if the war against the Axis powers was to be won.

Put that light out!

Oooops! Sorry!

The German bombs killed many people – but life for others went on.

At home people sheltered from bombs. They had to turn out all lights during the blackout or use blackout curtains.

We will never surrender…

Churchill's rousing speeches gave people hope.

Appearances by the King and Queen helped to keep morale high.

RATION BOOK

BUSINESS AS USUAL!

GROCER

BUTCHER

Food and other things, such as soap, were rationed. People queued and bought things with coupons from their ration books.

Shops carried on as usual, despite the bombing raids.

WWWRR!

WWWRRRR!

WWWRRRRRRR!

Get to the shelter! Don't run!

Oh no, not another air raid!

Who's got the cat?

Where else did people take shelter?

Many people used the street shelters and the Underground during an air raid. But more than half of the population preferred to risk staying at home. Some people used Anderson and Morrison shelters.

Street shelters were often very crowded during air raids.

Street shelters

These public shelters, made of brick and concrete, were built in major British towns and cities where air raids were most likely. The shelters were dry but not always very safe. A direct hit from a powerful bomb could still damage them.

London Underground stations

During heavy air raids, 79 London Underground stations became ready-made shelters for thousands of people. At night people slept on the platforms, and even between the train tracks when the power was off. The morning after a night-time raid people went home or to work. The stations were stuffy and smelly, so the government tried to improve some of them by adding beds, baths and canteens.

Liverpool had lots of shelters near the docks for the ship builders

Street shelters in Coventry saved many lives during heavy bombing

At the beginning of the Blitz, Winston Churchill used the disused Down Street Underground station near Hyde Park Corner as his own shelter, though at the time he discouraged the public from using the Underground.

Glasgow

Liverpool

Scampton

Coventry

Birmingham

Cardiff

Bicester

Larkhill

Plymouth

South East England

Duxford

Uxbridge

London

North Weald

Biggin Hill

- Heavily bombed city
- Major RAF airfield

Anderson shelters

Named after the Home Secretary, Sir John Anderson, these simple shelters were designed to be half-buried in gardens. To help them blend in, many owners grew flowers and vegetables on top! Although they were small, there was enough room for six people inside. Around 2 million Anderson shelters were made and they saved many lives during the Blitz.

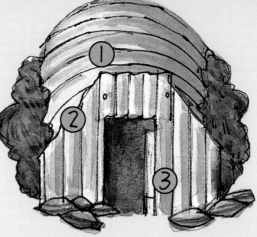

1. Roof made of corrugated metal and covered with earth
2. Arched roof design is very strong
3. Strong door made of corrugated metal. Narrow bunks inside could sleep six people

▲ Anderson shelters like this one were provided free to people earning less than £250 a year.

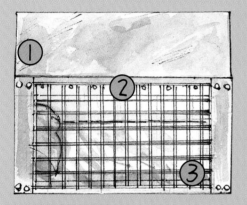

1. Solid steel plate designed to protect against falling debris
2. Strong wire mesh sides allow people inside to breathe
3. Could sleep two or three adults on the metal floor

Morrison shelters

These shelters, introduced in March 1941, were used inside the home. The steel sides and roof were strong enough to stay in one piece – even if a house collapsed – and the mesh protected against flying bricks and glass. At two metres long and one metre high, Morrison shelters were used as tables.

What was Hitler's bunker like?

Hitler's reinforced concrete bunker – the Führerbunker – was the biggest of many built under Berlin, Germany's capital city. It was 15 metres underground, with connecting stairs up to the government's Ministry of Foreign Affairs. Hitler moved into it in April 1945, as Soviet troops closed in and Germany awaited defeat.

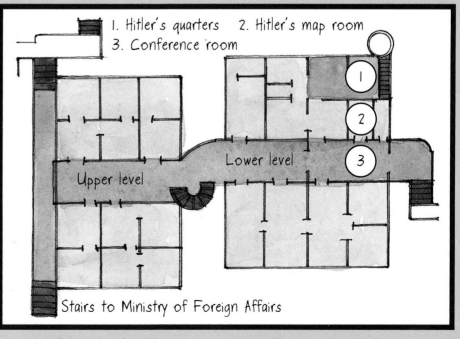

1. Hitler's quarters   2. Hitler's map room
3. Conference room

Upper level

Lower level

Stairs to Ministry of Foreign Affairs

▲ The Führerbunker had a six-metre thick reinforced concrete roof, meeting rooms and private rooms.

◎ How did the war end?

From 1943, German forces were struggling in many areas across Europe and North Africa. In May 1945, Germany finally surrendered. A few months later, a US plane dropped atom bombs on Japan, and Japan also surrendered. World War II ended on 14 August 1945.

1943 Axis forces under threat in North Africa and Europe.

1943 Italian forces retreat, and switch sides to fight Germany.

1943 Japanese forces losing ground in the Pacific.

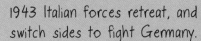

1944 Allied armies land in Normandy, France, in a fightback against Germany's occupation.

April 1945 Hitler commits suicide.

1945 Britain fights back against Japan in Burma (Myanmar).

7 May 1945 the end of war in Europe, after multinational forces (including British, Soviet and US soldiers) overrun Germany and the country surrenders.

14 August 1945 Japan surrenders after the USA dropped atom bombs on its cities Hiroshima and Nagasaki. The war finally ends.

By 1945, bombs had caused destruction in cities across Europe and the world. In Berlin, Germany's Reichstag parliament was a burnt shell. London had suffered terrible damage, too.

What is there left to see?

Post-war architects created imaginative buildings, and towers of glass and steel, to transform Berlin and London. But is there any evidence of the war remaining below the surface?

What happened to Hitler's bunker?

In December 1947 Soviet forces blew up Hitler's bunker and sealed it. It now lies underneath the garden of a Berlin apartment building. The site of the bunker had been filled in and built over for fear of it becoming a shrine to Hitler. In 2003, the German government handed the site to Jews, who had suffered under Hitler's rule.

What happened to the Cabinet War Rooms?

London's bunker, the Cabinet War Rooms, remained a World War II time capsule for nearly 40 years – sealed and preserved just as the wartime Prime Minister and his advisers left it. But from 1984 people have been able to follow in Churchill's footsteps, taking in the atmosphere and conditions of those dangerous war years underground. In 2005, the first ever museum dedicated to Winston Churchill opened in part of the basement that formed the Cabinet War Rooms.

▼ The Churchill Museum in London.

Displays throughout the museum show key events in Churchill's life

Audio equipment plays sounds from the war – including Churchill's speeches

Artefacts and other personal objects help to build up a picture of Churchill

Interactive timelines follow the whole of Churchill's life and World War II

▲ Entrance to the Cabinet War Rooms today.

27

◉ Timeline

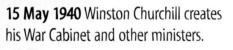

Mid-1930s Different bunker sites, including basements, are considered as the threat of war increases.

June 1938 The final site in Whitehall for the secure underground government bunker – the Cabinet War Rooms (CWRs) – is agreed on.

Sep 1938 The Munich Crisis. British Prime Minister (PM) Neville Chamberlain tries to talk peace with the German leader, Adolf Hitler.

27 Aug 1939 The CWRs bunker is ready.

1 Sep 1939 Germany invades Poland.

3 Sep 1939 Britain and France declare war on Germany. Churchill joins the Cabinet of Britain's current Prime Minister, Neville Chamberlain.

21 Oct 1939 Neville Chamberlain, the PM, holds the first meeting in the CWRs.

10 May 1940 Winston Churchill takes over from Neville Chamberlain as Britain's Prime Minister. He visits the CWRs.

15 May 1940 Winston Churchill creates his War Cabinet and other ministers.

July–Sep 1940 The Battle of Britain is fought between German and British air forces over southern England.

11 Sep 1940 Churchill makes his first important speech from the CWRs.

Sep 1940–May 1941 The Blitz. German planes drop 5,300 tons of bombs on London over 24 night-raids in September 1940. Shelters save many people.

15 Sep 1940 Battle of Britain Day – nearly 1,000 German planes cross the English coast. They suffer heavy losses against the RAF.

14 Nov 1940 German planes bomb Coventry, Liverpool and Birmingham.

May 1945 Germany surrenders.

Aug 1945 Japanese forces surrender in the Far East, and the war ends.

16 Aug 1945 The Cabinet War Rooms are no longer needed. Some rooms are kept exactly as they were left.

24 Jan 1965 Winston Churchill dies.

1981–4 The CWRs are preserved and restored.

2001 The President of the United States visits the CWRs.

2005 The Churchill Museum opens in the CWRs.

◎ Glossary

Allied forces
The combined forces of countries, including Britain, that fought against the Axis powers during World War II.

atom bomb
Developed during World War II, a bomb with huge explosive power. Also called a nuclear bomb.

Axis powers
The powers of Germany, Italy and Japan that fought against the Allies during World War II.

blackout
A time, especially during World War II, when streetlights and house lights were switched off. This made it more difficult for German bombers to find their targets. Blackout curtains were made of very thick material. When they were closed, people could safely have lights on.

Cabinet
A group of the most important members of the government. A War Cabinet is a group of ministers selected during a time of armed conflict.

conscripted
When someone is forced to join the military. At the outbreak of World War II many people in Britain signed up voluntarily, without being forced.

convoy
A group of ships travelling closely together. In the Atlantic during World War II convoys brought supplies of equipment to Britain from the USA. The convoys were made up of cargo ships, protected by Navy warships.

evacuated
When people are moved away from somewhere because it is dangerous. Children were evacuated from some cities during World War II because the cities were targets for German bombers.

morale
The feeling of confidence. During World War II many people were distressed at the loss of their homes or families. Events such as a tour by the King and Queen could cheer people up.

rationing
During World War II many goods were in very short supply. To buy anything in a shop, people used coupons from special ration books. People grew lots of food themselves because there were never enough coupons to last.

Soviet
From the Soviet Union (see next entry).

Soviet Union
The group of Communist countries in Eastern Europe and Northern Asia centred around Russia set up in 1922. The Union broke up in 1991.

Tube
The name given to the London Underground network because of the round-shaped tunnels.

U-boat
The name given to German submarines.

29

⊙ Index